Confidence

IS YOUR

SUPERPOWER

Confidence IS YOUR SUPER POWER

A Growth Mindset Book about Believing in Yourself and Trying New Things

WRITTEN BY
Leah Leynor, MA, LMFT

ILLUSTRATED BY
Zach Grzeszkowiak

ROCKRIDGE PRESS

For general information on our other products and services or to obtain technical support, please contact our Customer Care Department within the United States at (866) 744-2665, or outside the United States at (510) 253-0500.

Rockridge Press publishes its books in a variety of electronic and print formats. Some content that appears in print may not be available in electronic books, and vice versa.

Series Designer: Angie Chiu
Interior and Cover Designer: Regina Stadnik
Art Producer: Sara Feinstein
Editor: Erum Khan, Sasha Henriques
Production Editor: Holland Baker
Production Manager: Riley Hoffman

Illustrations © Zach Grzeskowiak, 2021
Author photo courtesy of Evan Pike Photography.

Paperback ISBN: 978-1-63878-226-1
eBook ISBN: 978-1-63878-284-1
R0
Printed in China

This book is dedicated to my family.
I am grateful for all their love and
support each and every day.

Everyone is born with a superpower. Many have more than one superpower.

Carlos and Clara are best friends. They have a superpower called confidence!

Feeling confident is awesome! We can all feel confident when we try new things, feel good about ourselves, and are proud.

Confidence means knowing that you can learn and try new things.

When you feel confident, you might raise your hand in school to answer a question because you know the answer.

Confidence is also feeling happy with yourself, being brave, and knowing you can do what you set your mind to!

Confidence is an important superpower!

When you feel confident, you do your best, feel good about yourself, and want to try new things.

Once confidence is your superpower, you can feel happy and proud of yourself every day.

What makes you feel proud or good about yourself when you try something new?

What do you like most about trying something new with a friend? What do you like least about it?

A parent or trusted grown-up can give you confidence when they help you learn to tie your shoes. When they show how they twist the laces together, you learn something new. When you try it yourself, they cheer you on, and you can feel confident!

How do you feel when a grown-up helps you learn something new?

What are some other activities you think a grown-up could help you with?

Sometimes it is easy to be confident. Other times being confident takes thought and hard work.

We can feel confident when we learn new things and ask for help. Sometimes we make mistakes, but we try again. If we do not feel confident yet, we can learn how!

Do you like it when you try something new?

What worries you the most about making a mistake?

Everyone is different. It means we can learn from each other. That way, we all feel good about ourselves.

Carlos and Clara know that when they feel happy and use their confidence superpower, they can help others feel good, too! Let's see how they practice doing their best every day.

How do you feel when you learn something new from someone different from you?

When did you help a friend feel confident about themselves?

Carlos thought he knew the answer to his teacher's question, but he worried that he might not be right.

He looked across the room and saw Ming raise her hand. Carlos wondered if Ming knew the answer.

Carlos decided to raise his hand even though he was not sure. Trying his best made Carlos feel confident.

How did Carlos use confidence when he wasn't sure if he had the right answer?

How do you feel about trying again if you don't get something right on your first try?

Clara asked her dad how to set the table for dinner.
Clara had never done it before, but she wanted to learn.

Clara felt happy and confident while her dad showed her how to set the table. She liked learning something new and being helpful.

How did Clara use her confidence to ask for help learning something new?

How do you feel about asking a grown-up to teach you something you have not done before?

Carlos was having a playdate outside with his friend Luke. Carlos and Luke decided they wanted to try the monkey bars.

Luke was a little nervous to try something new in front of his friend. Carlos cheered him on so he felt brave enough to try anyway!

How did Luke use confidence to try something new with his friend?

How confident do you feel about trying something for the first time in front of a friend?

Clara was riding bikes with her friend Leyla.

Leyla had never ridden without training wheels before. When Leyla tried to ride, she lost her balance and fell off her bike.

Leyla was not hurt. Clara reminded her that falling was okay. She hadn't learned to ride her bike yet, but she would keep trying.

How did Leyla use confidence when riding the bike without training wheels?

How confident do you feel learning something new if it does not work out the first time?

Carlos wanted to give water to his dog, Remi. When Carlos picked up the water bowl, he spilled water on the floor. At first, Carlos was upset.

Then Carlos realized he could use a water pitcher to pour better. Carlos liked that his mistake helped him learn how to do it better next time.

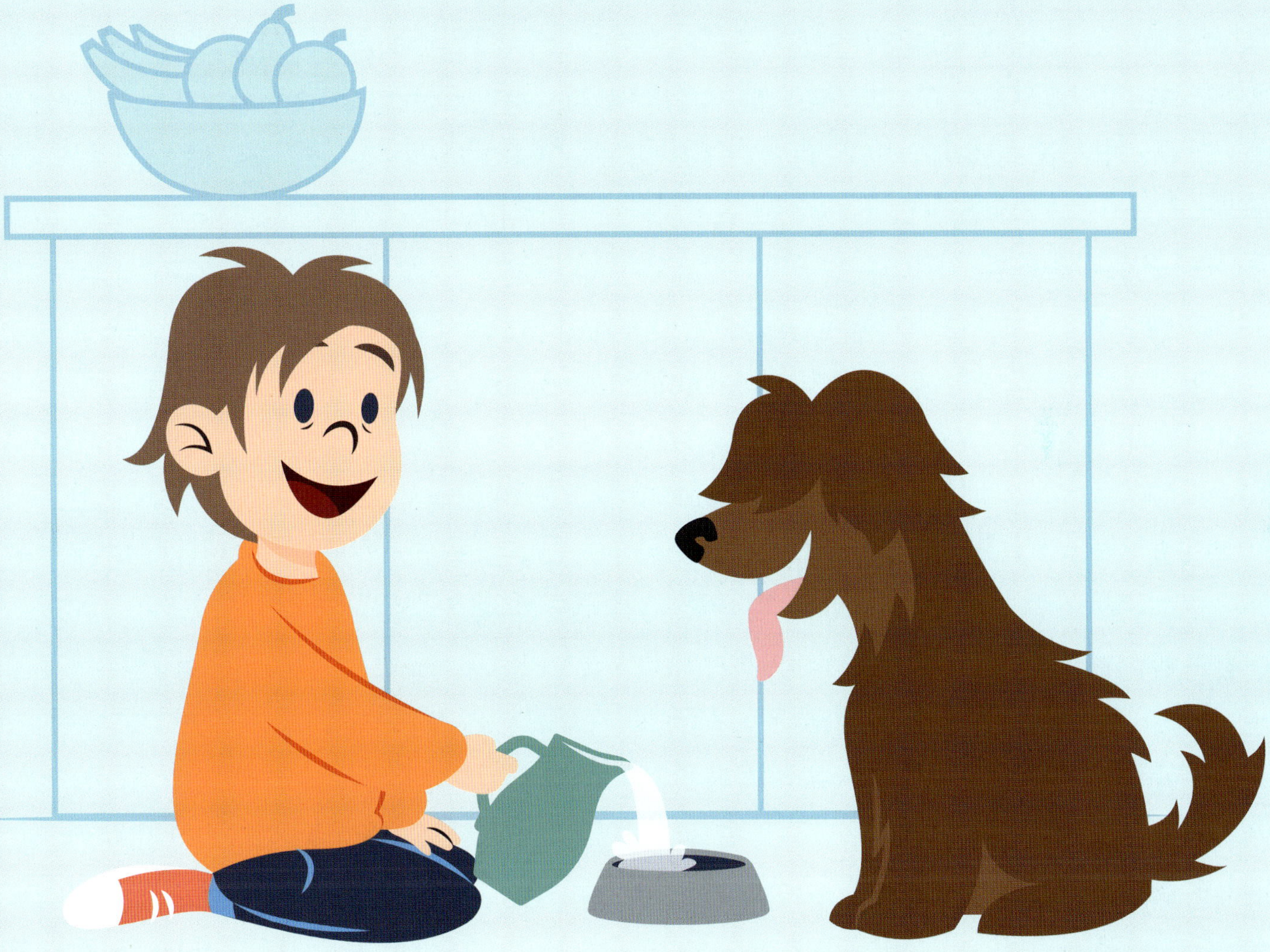

How did Carlos use confidence when realizing he made a mistake?

How does it feel to learn from your mistakes and try again?

Guillermo and Carlos were searching for hidden treasure. Guillermo was in charge of the treasure map.

Guillermo suddenly felt nervous. He realized the map was upside down and he needed to fix it.

Carlos helped his friend turn the map around. Together, they found the hidden treasure.

How did Guillermo use his confidence when he realized the map was upside down?

How do you feel when you correct a mistake?

Clara and her friend Grace wanted to help their class. Clara asked their teacher if they could hand out napkins for their afternoon snack.

Clara felt confident that their friends would be happy to have a napkin with their food. Clara and Grace both felt good when their teacher said yes.

Together, they got to work handing out napkins.

How do you think Clara's friends felt about her help?

How do you enjoy helping others? What do you think when you see others helping people?

Carlos and his mom talked about how it feels good to be kind.

Carlos wanted to bring his neighbor Mateo a get-well card because he was sick. Carlos sat down and colored a cheery card to bring to Mateo.

Carlos felt good about being kind to his friend.

How confident do you think Carlos felt when he was kind to his neighbor?

What are some ways you are kind to other people? How does it feel to be kind?

Carlos and Clara wanted to build a play fort together. They had never built one before.

They decided to make one out of cardboard boxes and blankets—but it fell down! Together, they said out loud, "I will keep trying. I am always learning. I like challenges."

They would build another fort.

What special reminders did Carlos and Clara give themselves while trying something new?

What helpful phrases do you tell yourself when you try something new?

Confidence helped Carlos and Clara feel proud and good about themselves. It also helped others feel the same!

Luke tried the monkey bars at the park with Carlos.

Leyla practiced riding her bike without training wheels every day.

Mateo made up new games all his friends could play together.

When we are confident, we can try new things and make mistakes. Then we can improve and try again. We can also cheer on a friend when they are nervous.

Confidence is a great superpower. It helps us feel like we can do what we set our mind to do!

How did Clara and Carlos use confidence as their superpower?

What would you do if you made a mistake? Would you feel confident trying again?

for PARENTS, EDUCATORS, *and* CAREGIVERS

Confidence Superpower Practice!

Tips and Activities That Help Kids Believe in Themselves and Try New Things

Confidence is an important superpower for adults and children alike! When children feel confident, not only do they feel happier and better about themselves, but they also feel less fearful and anxious. When any individual feels confident, they can learn new things and start over after making a mistake. With a stronger sense of personal confidence and motivation, a child will feel increased self-assurance and an enhanced ability to pursue whatever accomplishments they set their mind to.

The activities in this section give adults ideas to help children build their confidence superpower skills with practice, support, and encouragement. When we provide children with the skills to feel confident, we are also enabling them to make mistakes, learn, and grow. Increased confidence in children can also lead to positively improved interpersonal relationships because they may feel less anxious, more self-confident, and more relaxed, and will have increased empathy for others.

Caption in Time

In this activity, you will help your child find a photo of a time when they felt happy and confident (e.g., their first time riding a bike). This will help your child remember a time when they tried something new. Maybe they failed at first and needed to try again but succeeded in the end. You can also remind your child that they can accomplish any goal they set their mind to doing, even if at first they don't succeed.

Superpower Practice!

First, help your child choose a photo of themselves. In the photo, they could be trying something new, improving if they make a mistake, and/or eventually accomplishing their goal.

Then help your child choose a place to display the photo that is visible to them anytime they would like to see it and remind themselves of feeling confident.

Discussion Questions

How does it feel to try something new for the first time?

Why do you think it is important to learn from a mistake and try again?

How does it feel when someone encourages you because they know you can do it?

When you first saw the photo of yourself doing something you're proud of, how did you feel?

What is your favorite part of trying something new? What is your least favorite?

A Special Rock

In this activity, you can spend some quality time with your child by taking a walk together while looking for a special rock. You can explain to your child that we all have times when we feel doubtful, worried, or afraid, but sometimes we feel more confident and less anxious when we have something solid to hold on to.

Superpower Practice!

Encourage your child to pick out a rock that feels special to them. Help them look for it, and ask them questions about what they think is special. Discuss scenarios in which having their rock nearby might be helpful (e.g., in their backpack on the first day of school).

Discussion Questions

What does it feel like to know you have a special rock with you when need it?

Why do you think it is important to have things that help us feel less afraid?

What makes you feel special?

What makes your rock special to you?

What else could you try next time you feel nervous or anxious?

My Strengths!

In this activity, you will help your child list at least 10 things they are good at. Discuss the importance of knowing their strengths and what makes them different and special. You can also ask them to draw pictures around their list, which can help them visualize things they are good at doing.

Superpower Practice!

While sitting with your child, help them with their list by suggesting things you already know they are good at doing. Encourage your child to make the list their own with drawings and colors that appeal to them. You can also support your child by giving them a high five each time they add to their list.

Discussion Questions

Which thing on the list are you the best at doing?

Which strength are you most the proud of and why?

What makes you special?

What would your friends say makes you special?

How could you help a friend know that they are special, too?

Superpower Mottos

Ask your child to help you find five simple quotes about confidence. Write them on a poster board or a whiteboard to encourage your child to feel confident when they read the quotes. This can help them increase their positive inner dialogue and create a confidence reference tool.

Superpower Practice!

Help your child look through books or on the internet for simple quotes that they can write on their poster board or whiteboard. Encourage them to add bright colors that make them happy. They can even come up with their own mottos and add drawings to go with the sayings, too!

Discussion Questions

How does it feel to have a motto to use when you need a little more confidence?

Why do you think it is important to have a motto?

How does it feel when you use a motto to encourage someone else?

When you've used a motto to encourage yourself, how did you feel?

Which is your favorite motto? Why?

Special Time

Let your child know they are special! Tell them that you will spend 10 to 15 minutes with them every day engaging in an activity that they choose, such as drawing, playing a game, or preparing a snack. Allowing them to choose the activity will help them develop more independence and strengthen their decision-making. It will also validate that they are special, valued, and capable.

Superpower Practice!

Once you choose your special activity, help your child choose a place where you can meet at your agreed-upon time. For example, you can sit together in a reading corner with a book or at a table while coloring a creative picture. Each day, your child could choose a different activity to do while getting an adult's undivided attention.

Discussion Questions

How does it feel to choose the activity you want to do?

Why do you think it is important to spend special time with others?

How does it feel when you allow someone else to choose the activity you do?

When it was your special time, how did you choose the activity?

What is your favorite part of special time? What is your least favorite?

The Kindness Game

In this activity, you will help your child build their self-confidence and the confidence of others. All you have to do is go around the table during mealtime and say one kind thing about each person at the table. This activity can help your child build their self-confidence by hearing positive things about themselves from others. They'll also learn how to increase the self-confidence of others when they say kind words in return.

Superpower Practice!

Engage your child in this activity early on, either by letting them help prepare the meal in the kitchen or by having them set the table before you all sit down. During meal-preparation time, you can practice the kind things they might say to someone else at the table. They can then confidently tell someone else the things that they like about them without feeling put on the spot.

Discussion Questions

How does it feel to hear what someone likes about you?

Why do you think it is important to know what others like about you?

How does it feel to say kind words to someone else?

How difficult was it to tell someone else what you like about them?

What is your favorite part about the kindness game? What is your least favorite?

Magic Garden

In this activity, you will help your child gather the items needed to plant a small indoor garden. Through this activity, you can encourage your child to feel capable and increase problem-solving skills. Helping them create an ongoing responsibility can increase their confidence when they know they can do it!

Superpower Practice!

Help your child create a list of items they need to plant their garden and for their ongoing responsibility to help the garden grow. Encourage them to plant seeds of the plant they would like to grow. They can post a list of responsibilities near the garden to help remind them of what task comes next.

Discussion Questions

How does it feel when you see your garden grow?

Why do you think it is important to have responsibilities?

How does it feel to plant a garden?

What made you choose certain plants for your garden?

What do you like most about growing a garden?

Resources

ChildMind.org
The Child Mind Institute is an online resource with articles and research information for parents, teachers, and caregivers focused on the mental health of children.

ConfidentParentsConfidentKids.org
Confident Parents Confident Kids is an online resource for parents interested in encouraging and supporting their child's social and emotional development and mental health.

InstituteOfChildPsychologyConference.com
The Institute of Child Psychology is an online resource focused on children's mental health for parents, professionals, and caregivers.

***Kid Confidence* by Eileen Kennedy-Moore**
Kid Confidence is a book geared toward caregivers to help guide them in building self-esteem.

***Raising Good Humans* by Hunter Clarke-Fields, MSAE**
Raising Good Humans is a book for parents that promotes positive parenting strategies to raise kind, confident, and compassionate children.

***The Self-Driven Child* by William Stixrud, PhD, and Ned Johnson**
The Self-Driven Child is a book for parents to encourage their child's independence, choices, and engagement in new things.

***The Whole-Brain Child* by Daniel J. Siegel, MD, and Tina Payne Bryson, PhD**
The Whole-Brain Child is a book aimed at helping parents understand their growing child's mind in order to facilitate happier children with positive social, emotional, and mental health.

***The Whole-Brain Child Workbook* by Daniel J. Siegel, MD, and Tina Payne Bryson, PhD**
This is a workbook for parents to reflect and think about the positive life strategies to assist their child's development.

Acknowledgments

Thank you to my spouse, Michael, for reading my initial drafts and keeping the family fed by preparing meals so I could keep writing. For this, I am thankful. Special thanks to both Erum Khan, a positive editor, and Joshita Jain, a very encouraging acquisitions editor, from the Callisto Media team who both waited patiently for writing submissions. Finally, thanks to Tony Delmedico, PhD, LMFT, an awesome clinical supervisor, and to Pedro Ardiles-Arce, the best life/career mentor—I am eternally grateful for all the advice, support, and encouragement over the years, as I would not have accomplished what I have without either of you.

About the Author

Leah Leynor, MA, LMFT, provides a variety of counseling services to families and individual children, teens, and adults in Cary, North Carolina. She holds a master's degree in marriage and family therapy from Pfeiffer University, a massage therapy diploma from the American and European Massage Clinic, and a bachelor's degree in political science from Rider University. She is a certified hypnotherapist with specialized training in trauma counseling and family systems. She is a proud member of the American Association for Marriage and Family Therapy (AAMFT) and the North Carolina Association for Marriage and Family Therapy (NCAMFT). Leynor is the owner of Life Learning Counseling, PLLC (LifeLearningCounseling.com), Reliant Practice, LLC (ReliantPractice.com), and The Therapist In The Attic (TheTherapistInTheAttic.com).

About the Illustrator

Zach Grzeszkowiak is a graphic designer and illustrator originally from the Chicagoland area. He creates both digital and printed marketing materials like logos, infographics, and catalogs. In addition to his responsibilities as a designer, Zach also enjoys illustrating, animating, and sculpting colorful and exciting characters. Some of his favorite things to draw are animals and spooky creatures. He is constantly improving his skill set by drawing every day and experimenting with new mediums to work with. His favorite types of projects to work on involve educating, storytelling, and promoting positive change. To him, there's nothing quite as rewarding as using your talents and strengths to help a cause that you care deeply about.